CAPRICORN

HOROSCOPE

& ASTROLOGY

2025

Mystic Cat

Suite 41906, 3/2237 Gold Coast HWY

Mermaid Beach, Queensland, 4218

Australia

islandauthor@hotmail.com

Copyright © 2024 by Mystic Cat

Time set to Coordinated Universal Time Zone (UT±0)

All rights reserved. This book or any portion thereof may not be reproduced or used in any manner without the publisher's express written permission except for the use of brief quotations in a book review.

The information accessible from this book is for informational purposes only. None of the data should be regarded as a promise of benefits. It should not be considered a statutory warranty or a guarantee of results achievable.

Images are used under license from Fotosearch & Dreamstime.

Contents

January	16
February	24
March	32
April	40
May	48
June	56
July	64
August	72
September	80
October	88
November	96
December	104

Hello there,

Let me explain why my horoscope books may give different readings for each zodiac sign. The sky is always bustling with astrological activity, and I want to focus on what's most important for each star sign.

Every zodiac sign is unique, and the planets up above affect them differently. When I create horoscopes, I pay extra attention to the most critical astrological events for a specific sign. Some days, there might be lots of stuff happening in the stars, but one thing stands out as the essential factor for a particular zodiac sign.

I also consider which planet rules a sign and its associated element. This in-depth consideration helps me tailor my interpretations to match a sign's characteristics.

Ultimately, my goal is to provide you with unique advice and insights that match the cosmic influences for your sign. By focusing on what makes each sign special, I hope to help you understand yourself better and navigate the energies around you. Embracing your sign's strengths and challenges is the key to making my horoscopes feel uniquely aligned for you.

Cosmic Blessings,

Sia Sands

CAPRICORN 2025 HOROSCOPE & ASTROLOGY

Four Weeks Per Month

Week 1 – Days 1 - 7

Week 2 – Days 8 - 14

Week 3 – Days 15 - 21

Week 4 – Days 22 – Month-end

CAPRICORN

Dates: December 22nd to January 19th

Zodiac Symbol: Goat

Element: Earth

Planet: Saturn

House: Tenth

Color: Dark Green

Capricorn is the tenth astrological sign in the zodiac and belongs to the Earth element. People born under the Capricorn sign are known for their disciplined, practical, and ambitious nature. The symbol of Capricorn, the sea goat, represents a blend of terrestrial and aquatic energies, symbolizing the ability to navigate both the material and emotional realms.

Capricorn individuals have a strong sense of responsibility and determination, and they focus on achieving their goals. They are often willing to work hard and patiently to reach their desired outcomes. Ruled by Saturn, the planet of structure and discipline, Capricorns possess a sense of duty and a desire for stability.

Capricorn is located in the Tenth House of the zodiac and is associated with career, achievements, and public recognition. This placement emphasizes Capricorn's drive for success, commitment to professional endeavors, and desire to leave a lasting legacy.

Dark green is often associated with Capricorn due to its connections with stability, growth, and ambition. This color reflects the grounded and determined qualities of Capricorn individuals.

Capricorn embodies responsibility, determination, and ambition. Those born under this sign are often willing to put in the effort and work diligently to achieve their goals. Their practical approach to life and focus on long-term success make them reliable and valuable contributors in their personal and professional lives.

The Chinese Zodiac is a system that assigns an animal sign to each year in a 12-year cycle, and each animal is associated with certain personality traits and characteristics.

The Year of the Snake, in particular, holds special significance within Chinese culture and is rich in symbolism.

2025

The Chinese Year of the Snake

Capricorns are known for their practicality, determination, and ambition. They possess a strong work ethic and often strive for success and accomplishment. When the Year of the Snake arrives, it introduces a blend of energies that can resonate with and challenge the Capricorn personality.

During this year, Capricorns might find themselves drawn to the Snake's qualities of introspection and transformation. Just as snakes shed their skin to grow, Capricorns could shed old habits or patterns that no longer serve their goals, allowing personal growth and evolution.

The Year of the Snake encourages Capricorns to utilize their strategic thinking and planning skills to navigate their path. It's a time for them to assess their goals and ambitions, considering the long-term implications of their actions, much like the Snake's calculated approach to movement.

Capricorns' disciplined nature aligns well with the Snake's determination. This year might inspire Capricorns to focus on achieving their aspirations through a systematic and well-thought-out approach, like the Snake's patient navigation through different terrains.

The Year of the Snake could encourage Capricorns to connect deeply in relationships. Just as snakes rely on their senses to understand their surroundings, Capricorns might find themselves attuned to the feelings and motivations of others, fostering more authentic connections.

While Capricorns are known for their practicality, the Year of the Snake invites them to explore their inner landscape even more. It doesn't mean abandoning their structured approach; instead, it's about combining their strategic thinking with a deeper understanding of their motivations and desires.

Ultimately, the Year of the Snake offers Capricorns an opportunity for personal growth and enhanced success. By tapping into the Snake's symbolism of shedding the old and embracing the new, Capricorns can refine their approach to achieving their goals, foster deeper connections, and continue to strive for excellence while embracing their evolving selves.

CAPRICORN 2025 HOROSCOPE & ASTROLOGY

JANUARY WEEK ONE

☽ The Moon's entrance into Capricorn ushers in a notable shift in your emotional landscape. Capricorn's energy is akin to a seasoned CEO taking charge of your feelings, urging you to establish goals and embrace a business-like approach to your emotions. During this period, you'll likely concentrate on your long-term plans and ambitions, ready to tackle challenges with a determined spirit.

● This New Moon grants you a fresh canvas and a palette of possibilities. It's an invitation to set intentions, particularly regarding your career and public image. Whether you're eyeing a new job, embarking on a significant project, or simply seeking a fresh perspective on your professional life, this is your celestial reset button.

♒ As the Moon transitions into Aquarius, get ready for a shift towards an independent and innovative emotional vibe. Aquarius' energy is akin to a cosmic rebel, encouraging you to break from conventions and fully embrace your individuality. During this lunar transit, let your abilities shine and take the spotlight.

JANUARY WEEK ONE

☀ Brace yourself for a celestial wave of romance and dreaminess as Venus pirouettes into Pisces. This cosmic ballet paints a mesmerizing aura over your love life. Pisces' energy whispers poetry into your relationships, inspiring you to embrace your inner artist and let your emotions become a masterpiece.

💧 Hold onto your cosmic surfboard because a tidal wave of intensity crashes when Mars faces off against Pluto. Your desires blaze like a supernova but beware of power struggles and the unveiling of hidden motives.

🌙 As the Moon gracefully pirouettes into Pisces, your emotional landscape transforms into a dreamscape. Here, daydreams become voyages to the stars, and intuition is your guiding star.

○ When the Sun forms a harmonious sextile with Saturn, it's a cosmic nod of recognition for your unwavering commitment and hard work. This celestial partnership brings structure and accomplishment.

🌙 As the Moon charges into Aries, imagine a cosmic ignition switch flipping on, igniting progress and action.

JANUARY WEEK TWO

☀ As Mercury gracefully glides into Capricorn, a pragmatic and strategic aura settles over your communications and thoughts. This cosmic transition encourages you to consider the practical aspects of your communication, paving the way for fruitful endeavors.

☾ With the Moon's entrance into Gemini, the atmosphere becomes ripe for social interactions and intellectual exploration. Your curiosity takes center stage, prompting you to engage in stimulating conversations and seek knowledge. This lunar influence encourages you to embrace versatility and adaptability, making it an ideal period for learning, networking, and sharing ideas.

☾ As the Moon transitions into Cancer, your emotional landscape gains prominence. The gentle tug of Cancer's energy directs your focus toward home and family, emphasizing nurturing experiences. This lunar shift encourages the cultivation of emotional bonds.

♂ Mars forming a harmonious trine with Neptune infuses actions with an enchanting and intuitive quality.

JANUARY WEEK TWO

⚡ The Sun's harmonious trine with Uranus sparks a sense of exhilaration and an appetite for change. You are open to new experiences and unconventional ideas, eager to break free from routine. This alignment encourages personal growth and innovation, empowering you to embrace the unexpected with confidence and enthusiasm.

🌕 The Full Moon takes center stage, illuminating the skies and casting a radiant glow on your accomplishments and aspirations. It's a pivotal moment of culmination, where you can bask in the spotlight of your achievements and reassess your direction. This Full Moon invites you to celebrate your successes and make any necessary adjustments to align with your goals.

🌙 As the Moon later glides into charismatic Leo, your desire for attention and self-expression intensifies. You radiate confidently and creatively, seeking opportunities to showcase your unique talents.

✨ Venus squaring Jupiter brings a desire for indulgence and pleasure. It's a gentle reminder to savor life's pleasures in moderation.

JANUARY WEEK THREE

◊ The Sun's opposition with Mars ignites a cosmic battle of wills. Your drive and ambitions clash with external forces, leading to a potential tug-of-war. It's a test of patience and self-control, urging you to find a harmonious balance between assertion and diplomacy.

☽ As the Moon gracefully moves into Virgo's pragmatic domain, you'll gravitate toward practicality and detail-oriented tasks. This lunar influence encourages organization, self-care, and a focus on health matters.

⚡ The Sun's harmonious sextile with Neptune adds a touch of dreaminess to your existence. Imagination and intuition are heightened, making it an ideal time to explore your creative side and engage in spiritual pursuits.

♥ Venus's conjunction with Saturn brings a sense of commitment and seriousness to your relationships and finances. It's a cosmic reminder to take your romantic and financial matters seriously, laying a stable foundation for both.

JANUARY WEEK THREE

☽ As the Moon transitions into Libra, the cosmic emphasis shifts towards harmony and partnership. You'll seek balance in your interactions and be drawn to activities that promote beauty and diplomacy.

☿ Mercury forms harmonious sextiles with both Saturn and Venus, enhancing your communication skills and encouraging meaningful conversations. It's a favorable time for negotiations, making important decisions, and expressing your feelings clearly.

☼ The Sun enters the visionary realm of Aquarius, signaling a period of innovative thinking and a focus on community and humanitarian endeavors. It's a time to embrace individuality and work towards your unique goals.

● The Sun's conjunction with Pluto signifies a profound transformation and empowerment. It's a moment of rebirth, where you shed old layers of yourself to reveal a more authentic and empowered version.

☽ As the Moon shifts into Scorpio's intense energy, emotions run deep. You'll delve into your innermost feelings and desires to uncover hidden truths.

JANUARY WEEK FOUR

⚡ When Mars forms a sextile with Uranus, you'll feel a refreshing surge of energy and the desire for change. It's like a cosmic battery recharge, encouraging you to take bold actions that align with your individuality.

🗣 However, as Mercury opposes Mars, you might encounter challenges in communication and conflicts of interest. Patience and diplomacy will be your allies during this celestial clash.

☿ Mercury's trine with Uranus brings brilliance to your thoughts and ideas. Your mind is open to unconventional concepts and unique solutions.

☾ The Moon's ingress into adventurous Sagittarius inspires a thirst for knowledge and new experiences.

💚 Venus trine Mars adds a touch of romance and passion to your relationships. It's a harmonious cosmic dance that encourages balanced connections and shared desires.

☾ As the Moon moves into practical Capricorn, your focus shifts towards long-term goals. You'll be determined to build a solid foundation.

JANUARY WEEK FOUR

🌙 As the Moon joins Mercury in Aquarius, your emotions align with your intellectual pursuits. You'll seek emotional detachment and a sense of freedom.

✹ Mercury's conjunction with Pluto brings depth and intensity to your thoughts and conversations. You're not afraid to explore the depths of your psyche and engage in profound discussions.

● The New Moon marks a fresh start and an opportunity to set new intentions. It's like a cosmic blank canvas, inviting you to manifest your desires and dreams.

🔄 Uranus turning direct signals a shift towards progress and innovation in your life. Embrace change and be open to unexpected opportunities.

🌙 The Moon's ingress into Pisces enhances your empathy and intuition. It's a time to connect with your spiritual side and tap into your compassionate nature.

♎ The Sun's trine with Jupiter brings optimism and expansion. You'll feel generous and a desire to grow.

FEBRUARY WEEK ONE

💜 When Venus, the planet of love and beauty, aligns with dreamy Neptune, it's as if the cosmos orchestrates a mesmerizing symphony for your heart. Love and romance take on a thoughtful and ethereal quality during this celestial rendezvous, urging you to embrace your inner poet and express affection with flair. This aspect invites you to explore love's mystical and enchanting facets, transcending the ordinary and diving into the ocean of emotions with grace and sensitivity.

🌙 As the Moon gracefully strides into fiery Aries, your emotions catch fire with passion and assertiveness. This lunar transit encourages you to embrace your inner warrior and fearlessly charge into the world.

💬 Mercury's harmonious trine with Jupiter creates a balance between intellect and aspirations. This cosmic alliance fuels your curiosity and encourages you to seek out knowledge and share your insights with enthusiasm.

🌙 As the Moon moves into sensual Taurus, your emotions find solace in earthly delights. This lunar shift invites you to indulge your senses, savoring the sensual pleasures and basking in the moment's serenity.

FEBRUARY WEEK ONE

🌿 With Venus's ingress into Aries, your affections are bold, and you radiate self-confidence, making you a magnetic force in love and personal expression. This celestial shift encourages you to embrace your desires with a fearless spirit.

⏩ Jupiter's direct motion signals forward momentum and growth. After a phase of reflection and revision, projects and plans that may have been on hold can now progress with renewed vigor. Jupiter's expansive influence encourages you to reach new heights and seize opportunities for personal and professional expansion.

🌙 The Moon's transition into chatty Gemini invites social interactions and sparks intellectual curiosity. Your communication skills shine, and you'll enjoy exchanging ideas and exploring diverse perspectives.

💜 Venus's sextile with Pluto adds intensity to relationships and desires. This passionate and transformative energy invites you to explore the profound and mysterious aspects of your connections. It's a cosmic invitation to foster intimate bonds and experience the power of love's transformational magic.

FEBRUARY WEEK TWO

☽ As the Moon gracefully glides into nurturing Cancer, your emotions take on a tender and compassionate tone. You'll feel a deep connection to home and family, prioritizing comfort and moments of emotional nourishment. This cosmic transition encourages acts of kindness and a focus on your inner world.

◯ The Sun's conjunction with Mercury marks a period of mental clarity and effective communication. Your thoughts align seamlessly with your words, making it an excellent time for expressing yourself with precision and confidence. This celestial alignment invites you to engage in meaningful conversations and share your ideas with clarity.

◌ Mars forms a harmonious trine with Saturn, infusing your actions with discipline and determination. Pursuing your goals with steadfast focus and a systematic approach is like a cosmic green light. This celestial aspect encourages you to take concrete steps toward your ambitions and build a solid foundation for future endeavors.

FEBRUARY WEEK TWO

⚡ The Sun's square with Uranus ushers in an electrifying period of change and unpredictability. It's as if the cosmos is challenging you to break free from routine and embrace your individuality. Be prepared for unexpected events and opportunities pushing you out of your comfort zone.

● The Full Moon shines a spotlight on your achievements and long-term goals. It's a time of culmination and reflection, where you can celebrate your successes and evaluate the direction you wish to pursue next.

🌙 As the Moon later transitions into meticulous Virgo, your focus shifts towards practical matters and attention to detail. You'll find satisfaction in organizing your surroundings and tackling tasks with precision.

● On Valentine's Day, Mercury gracefully enters Pisces, infusing your thoughts and communications with empathy and imagination. This cosmic shift encourages you to express your feelings sensitively and engage in heartfelt conversations. It's a favorable period for romantic gestures and connecting soulfully.

FEBRUARY WEEK THREE

☾ As the Moon dives into the depths of Scorpio, your emotions take on a more profound and penetrating quality. This lunar placement urges you to explore the hidden realms of your psyche and the world around you. You may find yourself delving into topics of mystery, psychology, or metaphysics as your intuition becomes more pronounced. Authenticity in your emotional experiences is paramount during this phase, as you're encouraged to confront deep-seated feelings and transform them for the better.

☉ The Sun's gentle transition into compassionate Pisces ushers heightened sensitivity and artistic inspiration. Under this celestial influence, you'll feel a deeper connection to the collective consciousness and may find solace in creative or spiritual pursuits. Your empathy and imagination are enhanced, making it an ideal time for artistic expression, selfless acts of kindness, and a greater understanding of the human experience. Pisces season invites you to embrace your intuitive and compassionate nature, radiating warmth and knowledge to those around you.

FEBRUARY WEEK THREE

As the Moon embarks on a journey through adventurous Sagittarius, optimism and a thirst for exploration permeate your emotional landscape. During this lunar phase, you're naturally drawn to new experiences, whether physical travel or a philosophical journey of the mind. Your sense of adventure is ignited, and you'll seek opportunities to broaden your horizons and gain fresh perspectives. Freedom becomes a cherished value, and you're likely to engage in activities that allow you to stretch your boundaries and expand your knowledge.

Mercury's square with expansive Jupiter amplifies your communication and thinking processes, infusing them with enthusiasm and grand ideas. While this alignment fosters a visionary mindset and encourages big thinking, it's essential to maintain a sense of practicality. Avoid the trap of overcommitting or making promises that may be challenging to fulfill. Instead, balance your expansive thinking and the need for realistic planning. Harness the optimism of Jupiter to fuel your ambitions while keeping your feet firmly on the ground.

FEBRUARY WEEK FOUR

🌙 When the Moon gracefully steps into the disciplined realm of Capricorn, your emotions take on a structured and goal-oriented tone. It's a phase where you'll find comfort in setting practical objectives and working steadily toward your ambitions. Your focus on responsibilities and long-term plans intensifies, and you may be drawn to take on leadership roles or tackle tasks that require your unwavering dedication. This lunar influence encourages you to create a stable emotional foundation, making it an excellent time for life planning.

🔴 Mars, the cosmic warrior, turns direct, signaling a significant shift in how you channel your energy and assertiveness. After introspection, you'll feel a surge of forward momentum and a renewed sense of motivation. This cosmic change empowers you to pursue your goals with increased vigor and determination, breaking free from any previous obstacles that held you back.

💬 Mercury's conjunction with Saturn brings a serious and structured tone to your thoughts and conversations. During this cosmic alignment, your mental faculties are sharp, and you approach discussions methodically and cautiously.

FEBRUARY WEEK FOUR

The Moon's ingress into dreamy Pisces ushers in heightened sensitivity and emotional receptivity. You'll feel more connected to the subtle undercurrents of emotions, making it an excellent time for artistic expression, spiritual pursuits, and deep introspection. Your compassion shines during this lunar phase, and you may find solace in acts of kindness and self-care.

Mercury's sextile with innovative Uranus adds a touch of spontaneity and open-mindedness to your mental processes. Your thoughts are agile and receptive to unconventional ideas, making it an excellent time to brainstorm, experiment, and explore new concepts. This cosmic aspect encourages breakthroughs in your thinking and communications, allowing you to approach problems with fresh and inventive solutions.

The New Moon heralds the start of a new lunar cycle, a blank canvas upon which to set fresh intentions and initiate new projects. It's a potent moment for setting goals, especially those related to creativity, dreams, and intuitive insights. As the Moon renews, consider the seeds to plant and the intentions you wish to manifest.

MARCH WEEK ONE

💔 Venus's retrograde journey invites you to revisit matters of the heart and reassess your values in relationships and finances. It's like a cosmic rewind button, allowing you to reflect on past romantic experiences and the things that truly matter to you. During this period, you may reevaluate your desires and seek greater authenticity in your connections.

💬 Mercury's conjunction with Neptune enhances your intuitive and imaginative faculties, turning your thoughts into a vivid tapestry of dreams and possibilities. It's as if your mind becomes a portal to a world of creativity and intuition, making this an ideal time for artistic and spiritual pursuits. Your communication takes on a compassionate and empathetic tone, allowing for meaningful conversations.

⚡ The Sun's square with expansive Jupiter infuses your life with enthusiasm and growth. While this cosmic connection can amplify your ambitions and optimism, it's essential to maintain a sense of balance and avoid overextending yourself. Use this cosmic energy to set achievable goals and expand your horizons with wisdom and an understanding of moderation.

MARCH WEEK ONE

☿ With Mercury's ingress into assertive Aries, your communication style becomes more direct as your thoughts are clear, and you're unafraid to express your opinions and ideas. This cosmic shift encourages you to take the initiative in your conversations and boldly pursue your intellectual interests.

☽ The Moon's entry into sensual Taurus brings a sense of stability and a desire for comfort and security. During this lunar phase, you'll find satisfaction in simple pleasures, such as enjoying a delicious meal or indulging in sensory experiences. It's a time to nurture your physical and emotional well-being.

☽ The Moon's transition into communicative Gemini sparks your curiosity and desire for social interaction. Your mind is agile and adaptable, making it excellent for engaging in conversations and gathering information.

☿ Mercury's sextile with transformative Pluto adds depth and intensity to your communication and thought processes. This celestial fusion encourages you to delve fearlessly into the profound realms of emotional connection.

MARCH WEEK TWO

☀ The Sun's harmonious trine with Mars ignites a powerful surge of energy and determination. You'll feel the drive to take action and confidently assert your desires. Pursuing your goals, making things happen, and embracing your power is a cosmic green light.

☽ As the Moon gracefully enters the charismatic sign of Leo, your emotions take on a dramatic and expressive quality. It's a time when you'll be drawn to the spotlight and seek recognition for your talents. Your inner performer shines; you may find joy in creative endeavors and entertaining others.

💬 Mercury's conjunction with Venus adds a touch of charm and grace to your communication. Your words are filled with warmth and diplomacy, making it a perfect time for pleasant conversations and harmonious interactions. You'll find it easier to express affection.

☽ The Moon's transition into detail-oriented Virgo encourages focusing on practical matters and organization. This lunar phase is ideal for decluttering, improving efficiency, and caring for your physical well-being.

MARCH WEEK TWO

☀ The Sun's conjunction with Saturn marks a period of increased discipline and responsibility. It's when you'll feel a strong sense of duty and a commitment to your long-term goals. While challenges may arise, your determination and perseverance help overcome them.

☀ The Full Moon shines a spotlight on your achievements and long-term aspirations. It's a moment to celebrate your successes and assess your progress toward your goals. Emotions run high during this phase, providing valuable insights into your ambitions.

⚡ The Sun's sextile with Uranus adds an element of excitement and innovation to your life. While maintaining a sense of structure and responsibility, you're also open to change and unexpected opportunities. Embrace your individuality and be prepared for fresh insights and breakthroughs.

☽ As the Moon continues its journey, entering the diplomatic sign of Libra, your focus turns to relationships and harmony. You'll be naturally inclined to seek balance in your interactions and create a pleasant and cooperative atmosphere.

MARCH WEEK THREE

🔄 Mercury's retrograde motion signals a time for introspection and review. During this cosmic phase, it's wise to double-check your plans, communication, and agreements. Delays and misunderstandings may arise, but these moments allow you to reevaluate your thoughts and ideas. It's a time to look back before moving forward with greater clarity.

🌙 As the Moon delves into Scorpio, your emotions take on an intense and passionate quality. It's when you'll feel the urge to uncover hidden truths and explore the depths of your feelings. You may find solace in solitude, introspection, and a desire to transform and release emotional baggage.

🌙 As the Moon continues its journey into adventurous Sagittarius, your emotions are infused with optimism and a desire for exploration. You'll be drawn to new experiences and a broader perspective, making this an excellent time for travel, learning, and expanding your horizons.

MARCH WEEK THREE

☀ When the Sun conjoins Neptune, your intuition and imagination soar to new heights. It's as if the boundaries between reality and dreams blur, allowing you to tap into your artistic and spiritual potential. This cosmic alignment encourages compassion, creativity, and a heightened connection to the mystical and ethereal realms.

☺ The Sun's transition into Aries marks the Vernal Equinox, a decisive moment of rebirth and new beginnings. It's a time when the energy of the cosmos propels you forward with fresh vitality and a pioneering spirit. The Aries season inspires you to take initiative and embrace your individuality.

☾ Venus's sextile with Pluto brings a touch of intensity and depth to your relationships and desires. It's a cosmic invitation to explore the transformative power of love and passion. You may be drawn to profound emotional connections and experiences that impact you. This aspect encourages you to delve into your desires with honesty and authenticity.

MARCH WEEK FOUR

☾ As the Moon gracefully transitions into Capricorn, you'll experience a shift in your emotional landscape. This lunar phase encourages a more pragmatic and disciplined approach to your feelings. You may focus on your responsibilities and long-term goals, seeking stability and structure.

♣ The conjunction of the Sun and Venus creates a celestial atmosphere of romance and harmony. It's as if the universe highlights the beauty in your relationships and the things that bring you joy. During this period, your interactions are infused with affection and a deep appreciation for all things lovely. It's the perfect time to express your feelings and revel in the finer aspects.

✦ The Sun's sextile with Pluto adds depth and intensity to your experiences. This cosmic connection encourages transformation and personal empowerment. You'll be able to delve into your desires, make meaningful changes, and step in your power.

☽ When the Moon moves into Aquarius, your emotions take on a more open and humanitarian quality. It's when your mind opens to new perspectives.

MARCH WEEK FOUR

💜 The conjunction of Venus and Neptune further amplifies the dreamy and romantic atmosphere. It's a period of heightened creativity and a strong desire to experience transcendent love and beauty. Your imagination soars, and you may be drawn to artistic and spiritual pursuits.

🌑 The New Moon marks a fresh beginning and an opportunity to set new intentions. This lunar phase invites you to plant the seeds of your desires and envision the future you wish to create. It's a moment of renewal and a cosmic blank canvas on which to paint your aspirations.

💬 Mercury's ingress into Pisces enhances your intuition and empathy in your communications. Your words become more compassionate and poetic, making it an ideal time for deep, heartfelt conversations. You'll find a natural ability to connect profoundly with others.

🔮 With Neptune's ingress into Aries, a new era of dreams and spiritual exploration begins. This cosmic shift may inspire innovative and idealistic visions for the future, fostering a sense of renewal and individuality.

APRIL WEEK ONE

☽ Transitioning into Cancer, the Moon deepens your emotions and nurtures your sense of home and security. This phase encourages you to connect profoundly with your feelings and loved ones. You'll feel a stronger desire to create a cozy and harmonious environment.

🪐 Saturn's sextile with Uranus creates a harmonious cosmic conversation that blends tradition with innovation. It's when you can incorporate new and forward-thinking approaches into your existing structures and systems, leading to increased stability and progress. This aspect offers a unique opportunity for positive change and evolution.

◉ When Mars sextiles Uranus, you're infused with energy and a desire for action. Taking bold, dynamic steps toward your goals is like a cosmic call. This aspect fosters courage and a willingness to embrace change with confidence.

✺ The trine between Mars and Saturn combines your drive with discipline, resulting in a harmonious balance of energy and focus. This cosmic alignment encourages efficient and purposeful actions.

APRIL WEEK ONE

☀ The Sun's sextile with Jupiter blesses you with optimism and expansion. It's as if the universe is opening doors to new opportunities and experiences. You'll find aligning your intentions with your higher purpose easier during this period.

💜 Venus's trine with Mars infuses your relationships with harmony and sensuality. This aspect creates a delightful balance between affection and desire, making it an ideal time for romantic endeavors. Your interactions with loved ones become more harmonious.

♍ When Venus meets Saturn in conjunction, it adds a touch of seriousness and commitment to your relationships and financial matters. This celestial union encourages you to take a more responsible approach to your connections and resources. It's a period for building solid foundations in the heart and finances.

☿ Mercury's direct motion signifies a turning point in your communication and decision-making. It's like the gears of your mind are shifting back into forward motion. With the challenges of the retrograde period behind you, you can now move with more clarity.

APRIL WEEK TWO

✦ When Venus forms a harmonious sextile with Uranus, your love life and creative endeavors receive fresh air. This aspect encourages you to break free from routines and embrace spontaneity. In your relationships, you might find excitement in exploring new experiences together, and when it comes to art and aesthetics, you'll be drawn to innovative and unconventional expressions of beauty. Infuse life with a touch of the extraordinary.

☾ The Moon's journey into practical Virgo invites you to embrace the details of your daily life. During this phase, your emotions become finely tuned to organization and efficiency. You'll likely have a keen eye for making improvements in your surroundings, whether it's decluttering or streamlining your routines.

💜 As the Moon transitions into Libra, the focus shifts to your relationships and the pursuit of harmony. This lunar phase acts like a cosmic peacemaker, encouraging you to seek balance in your interactions with others. You'll find beauty in compromise, and the desire for fairness and cooperation becomes prominent. It's an ideal time for socializing, resolving conflicts, and appreciating the elegance of life.

APRIL WEEK TWO

🌕 The Full Moon marks a significant climax and culmination in your life. It's a time for reflection, celebration, and letting go. Any efforts or intentions you've been working on are now illuminated, and you can see the results more clearly. Emotions may run high, so it's an excellent moment to release what no longer serves you and embrace the achievements and realizations that have come to fruition.

🌱 With Venus turning direct, the energy of love and beauty gains momentum. Any romantic or creative ventures that may have felt stalled during Venus's retrograde now move forward. You'll notice that your relationships regain a sense of flow and progression, and your art appreciation and the pleasures of life reawaken.

🌑 The Moon's ingress into Scorpio ushers in emotional depth and intensity. During this time, you may find yourself drawn to exploring life's mysteries and delving into the hidden realms of your psyche. Your intuition is heightened, making it an auspicious moment for introspection and transformation. This lunar phase invites you to embrace the shadows and navigate the depths of your soul with courage and curiosity.

APRIL WEEK THREE

💧 Mars's entry into Leo infuses your actions with drama and self-expression. You'll approach tasks and challenges with a flair for the theatrical, making it impossible to ignore your presence. This cosmic shift ignites your passions and encourages you to pursue your desires with confidence and boldness.

🌒 As the Moon moves into Capricorn, a sense of responsibility and determination washes over you. It's when you're driven to achieve your goals and take practical steps toward success. Your emotions align with your ambitions, making it an ideal period for setting clear intentions and working diligently toward them.

☉ The Sun's entrance into Taurus ushers in a period of stability and sensual pleasures. You'll find comfort in simple delights, from good food to beautiful surroundings. This solar phase encourages you to connect with the physical world and indulge in activities that engage your senses.

☼ Mars's trine with Neptune combines the energy of action with the subtlety of intuition. This aspect encourages compassion, kindness, and charity.

APRIL WEEK THREE

♥ Venus's sextile with Uranus adds a touch of excitement and unpredictability to your relationships. This celestial connection encourages you to embrace spontaneity and explore unique ways of connecting with others. It's a time when unexpected romantic or social opportunities may arise.

◪ Mercury's sextile with Pluto deepens your intellectual pursuits and conversations. You're drawn to profound topics and can uncover hidden truths. This aspect enhances your problem-solving skills and empowers you to make transformative changes through communication and research.

🜁 As the Moon moves into Aquarius, your emotions take on an innovative and open-minded quality. It's when you may feel a stronger sense of community and a desire to connect with like-minded individuals. Your humanitarian side shines, making it an ideal period for social activism and collaborative projects.

◊ The Sun's square with Mars creates an energetic tension. While it can spark motivation and drive, channeling this with purpose avoids impulsive actions.

APRIL WEEK FOUR

☀ As the Sun squares Pluto, you can confront deep-seated issues and power dynamics. This aspect can bring hidden tensions to the surface. It's a time for transformation and rebirth.

💜 Venus's conjunction with Saturn brings a sense of seriousness to your relationships and approach to love. It's a time when you may need to define boundaries and commitments. While this aspect can create a sense of responsibility in your interactions, it also brings stability and a focus on long-term partnerships.

🜄 When the Moon ventures into Aries, your emotions are ignited with passion and a desire for action. It's a time of impulsivity and a need for independence. You're driven by a pioneering spirit and a sense of courage, making it a great time to initiate new projects or pursue your goals with determination.

🜂 Mars opposing Pluto sets the stage for intense power struggles and confrontations. This cosmic clash can stir deep-seated tensions and challenge your desires. Use your energy wisely during this period, as impulsive actions may lead to regret.

APRIL WEEK FOUR

♣ As the Moon enters Taurus, your emotions become grounded and focused on the tangible aspects of life. You may seek comfort, stability, and a connection to nature. This lunar phase encourages you to savor life's pleasures and invest in your well-being.

● The New Moon represents a fresh start and the beginning of a new lunar cycle. It's a time for setting intentions and planting the seeds of your desires. This lunar phase encourages you to initiate new projects, make important decisions, and let go of what no longer serves your growth.

◯ When the Moon moves into communicative Gemini, your emotions take on a more social and curious quality. Your mind is agile and open to new information.

🐦 Venus's ingress into Aries ignites your love life with passion and a desire for spontaneity. You're more inclined to pursue your appetites with boldness and independence. In matters of the heart, you seek excitement and novelty, making this a time of romantic adventures and individual expression.

MAY WEEK ONE

💜 When Venus, the planet of love and beauty, conjoins Neptune, it's like a celestial symphony of romance and inspiration. This enchanting aspect infuses your relationships with dreamy, romantic qualities. You're more attuned to the subtler, more spiritual aspects of love, and your artistic and creative expression is heightened. This cosmic call is a time for deep emotional connections and a heightened appreciation of beauty in all its forms.

🦁 With the Moon's transition into Leo, your emotions take on a regal and expressive quality. You're ready to take center stage, and your feelings are magnified, demanding recognition and appreciation. This lunar phase encourages you to let your inner light shine and embrace individuality.

🔄 Pluto's retrograde motion marks a time of introspection and transformation on a deeply psychological level. It's as if the cosmic powerhouse Pluto turns its energy inward, allowing you to revisit and reevaluate the profound changes you've undergone. This period encourages you to address power dynamics, release old patterns, and find your inner strength.

MAY WEEK ONE

When Mercury sextiles Jupiter, your mental horizons expand, and your communication takes on an optimistic and enthusiastic tone. It's when you're eager to learn, share knowledge, and engage in meaningful conversations. Your ability to see the big picture and solve complex issues is enhanced.

As the Moon moves into Virgo, your emotions take on a practical and analytical nature. It's a phase when you seek order and organization in your surroundings and daily routines. You may find satisfaction in attending to details and improving efficiency.

Venus sextile Pluto adds intensity and depth to your relationships and creative pursuits. This celestial connection encourages profound emotional connections, transformation, and empowerment. You're drawn to experiences and people with a lasting impact, and your creative expression takes on a more profound and meaningful quality. This aspect enhances your ability to delve into the complexities of love and art. It's a time for nurturing connections and engaging in meaningful activities that speak to the depths of your soul.

MAY WEEK TWO

☀ As the Moon gracefully enters Libra, your emotions seek harmony, balance, and connection. You're drawn to social interactions and cooperative endeavors. This lunar phase encourages you to engage in diplomacy, seek fairness, and appreciate the beauty in your surroundings. It's a time when you value relationships and the shared experiences that unite people.

🌱 With Mercury's ingress into Taurus, your communication style becomes grounded and practical. Your words take on a tangible quality, and you may speak more deliberately and sensibly. This planetary transit is an excellent period for discussing finances and material possessions. It enables you to build a solid foundation for your ideas.

💀 The Moon's transition into Scorpio marks a phase of emotional intensity and transformation. You're delving deep into your inner world, exploring hidden emotions and desires. This lunar phase encourages you to embrace your power, investigate the mysteries of life, and let go of what no longer serves you.

MAY WEEK TWO

🌕 The Full Moon is a climax of emotional energy and illumination. It's a time when your intentions and projects peak, and you see the results of your efforts. Emotions run high during this phase, and it's a decisive moment to release what no longer aligns with your goals and aspirations.

🔍 When Mercury squares Pluto, your thoughts dive into the depths of psychological understanding and transformation. This aspect encourages you to uncover hidden truths and challenge superficial perspectives. It's a time when your words may carry a profound impact, but be mindful of potential power struggles in your communications.

🏔 As the Moon moves into adventurous Sagittarius, your emotions take on a more exploratory and open-minded quality. You're eager to expand your horizons, both mentally and physically. This lunar phase encourages you to seek new experiences, embrace a broader perspective, and tap into your natural curiosity. It's a time when you're drawn to travel, learning, and philosophical pursuits.

MAY WEEK THREE

☀ With the Moon's transition into structured Capricorn, your emotions take on a responsible and goal-oriented demeanor. You're inclined to focus on your long-term ambitions, seeking to create a sense of order and stability in your life. This lunar phase encourages you to set practical objectives and take steps toward achieving them.

⚡ The conjunction of the Sun and Uranus marks a time of exciting and unexpected developments. It's like a cosmic lightning bolt, electrifying your life with innovation and change. This cosmic aspect encourages you to embrace uniqueness, break free from limitations, and explore new horizons.

💧 Mercury's square with Mars ignites your mental processes and communication with fiery energy. This aspect can lead to intense discussions, debates, and impulsive reactions. It's essential to channel this energy constructively and avoid hasty decisions or confrontations. This aspect encourages you to think before you act and channel your energy into productive pursuits.

MAY WEEK THREE

◪ As the Moon glides into Aquarius, your emotions take on an independent and innovative quality. You're drawn to unconventional ideas and a sense of community. This lunar phase encourages you to express your individuality and engage in activities that promote social change and progress.

☉ The Sun's sextile with Saturn brings a sense of discipline and focus to your endeavors. It's when you can steadily progress toward your goals and responsibilities. This aspect encourages you to take a structured approach to your work and build a solid foundation for future success.

☾ With the Moon's transition into dreamy Pisces, your emotions become profoundly intuitive and sensitive. You may find yourself more in tune with your inner world and the feelings of others. This lunar phase encourages creativity, introspection, and a desire to connect on a spiritual or artistic level.

☀ The Sun's ingress into versatile Gemini marks a communicative phase. This solar shift encourages mental agility, socializing, and a thirst for knowledge.

MAY WEEK FOUR

☌ When the Sun forms a trine with Pluto, it's as if the cosmos supports profound transformation and empowerment. You have the energy and determination to make significant changes in your life, particularly in areas where you seek personal growth and renewal.

☉ Mercury's conjunction with Uranus brings a burst of mental innovation and a desire for fresh insights. Your mind is open to unconventional ideas, and you may experience sudden flashes of inspiration. This aspect encourages you to break free from mental routines and explore new possibilities.

♄ Saturn's ingress into Aries marks a shift in your approach to structure and responsibility. You may find yourself taking a more assertive and independent stance when it comes to your obligations and goals. It is a period of initiating new strategies and building foundations with confidence.

♊ Mercury's move into Gemini enhances your communication skills and curiosity. You become more friendly, adaptable, and mentally agile. It is an excellent time for networking, learning, and sharing ideas.

MAY WEEK FOUR

🌑 Mercury's sextile with Saturn promotes structured and practical thinking. It's a favorable aspect for making long-term plans, focusing on detailed tasks, and seeking advice from experienced individuals. This alignment encourages responsible and systematic decision-making.

🌑 The New Moon marks a fresh beginning and an opportunity to set new intentions. It's like a cosmic reset button, giving you a chance to plant the seeds of your desires. This lunar phase encourages introspection and the formulation of new goals.

🪐 Mercury's trine with Pluto intensifies your mental processes and investigative skills. You're drawn to deep, transformative conversations and research. This aspect encourages you to uncover hidden truths and make meaningful changes through communication.

☀️ The Sun's conjunction with Mercury enhances your ability to express yourself with clarity and purpose. Your mind and identity align, making it an excellent time for self-expression and intellectual pursuits. This aspect supports effective communication and mental focus.

JUNE WEEK ONE

♍ When the Moon gracefully enters Virgo, your emotions take on a practical and analytical tone. You become more detail-oriented and focused on the finer points of life. This lunar phase encourages organization and a desire for efficiency. It's an excellent time to address tasks that require precision and to attend to your well-being with a health-conscious approach.

♎ As the Moon moves into Libra, your emotions seek harmony and balance in your relationships and surroundings. You become more diplomatic and inclined to find compromises that foster peace and cooperation. This lunar phase encourages you to appreciate beauty and aesthetics, making it an excellent time for creative and artistic pursuits.

☽ Venus sextile Jupiter forms a delightful aspect that enhances your social and romantic life. It's like a cosmic blessing for love, pleasure, and abundance. This alignment encourages positive and enjoyable interactions with others, as well as the potential for financial or romantic opportunities.

JUNE WEEK ONE

🚀 Mercury sextile Mars ignites your mental processes with energy and drive. You're articulate and assertive in your communication, making it an excellent time for debates and discussions. This aspect encourages you to express your ideas with confidence and take action on your thoughts. This aspect promotes effective and passionate communication, making it an excellent time for lively discussions and problem-solving.

🌷 Venus's ingress into Taurus brings a sensual and grounded approach to love and aesthetics. You're drawn to comfort and luxury, appreciating the beauty in simple pleasures. This transit encourages you to indulge in sensory experiences and build a stable and affectionate foundation in your relationships.

🦂 As the Moon enters Scorpio, your emotions take on an intense and transformative quality. You're more in tune with your innermost feelings and may seek to uncover hidden truths. This lunar phase encourages self-reflection, healing, and a deep connection to the mysteries of life.

JUNE WEEK TWO

☀ Mercury's conjunction with Jupiter marks a time of expanded thinking and learning. Your mind is open to new ideas, and you have a hunger for knowledge. This aspect encourages positive thinking and effective communication of your beliefs and visions.

☾ Mercury's move into Cancer brings a more emotionally sensitive and nurturing tone to your communication style. You're likely to express yourself with greater empathy and care for others' feelings. This transit encourages heartfelt conversations and an increased focus on domestic and family matters.

● Mercury square Saturn can temporarily introduce mental challenges and delays. It's essential to approach your tasks with patience and precision during this period. While it may feel like a mental hurdle, it's an excellent time for careful planning.

▲ As the Moon enters Sagittarius, your emotions seek adventure and expansion. You're drawn to exploring new horizons, both mentally and physically. This lunar phase encourages you to embrace a more optimistic and open-minded perspective.

JUNE WEEK TWO

🏠 Jupiter's ingress into Cancer heralds a period of emotional growth and expansion in your personal life. You may experience increased blessings and opportunities related to home, family, and nurturing. This transit encourages you to seek comfort and security in your domestic environment.

🌕 The Full Moon is a time of culmination and release. It's like the peak of a lunar cycle, bringing matters to a head. This lunar phase encourages you to evaluate your progress, celebrate your achievements, and let go of what no longer serves you.

💌 Mercury sextile Venus enhances your communication skills and relationships. You'll find it easier to express affection and harmony in your interactions. This aspect encourages social charm and the ability to convey your feelings with grace and charm.

⛰️ As the Moon enters Capricorn, your emotions adopt a practical and ambitious tone. This lunar phase encourages you to take a structured and disciplined approach to your endeavors, seeking to climb the symbolic mountain of your ambitions.

JUNE WEEK THREE

⚡ Mars square Uranus creates an atmosphere of tension and unpredictability. It's like a cosmic clash between the warrior planet and the disruptor. This aspect encourages you to be cautious and flexible, as impulsive actions can lead to unexpected consequences.

♄ Jupiter square Saturn represents a cosmic tug of war between expansion and restriction. It's a time when you may feel the push and pull of wanting to grow and progress while also facing the realities of structure and responsibility. This aspect encourages finding a balance between optimism and practicality.

☾ As the Moon gracefully moves into Pisces, your emotions take on a dreamy and intuitive quality. It encourages introspection and a connection to the mystical realms. This lunar phase favors artistic and spiritual pursuits, as well as deep empathy for others.

⚒ Mars's ingress into Virgo brings a more systematic and detail-oriented approach to your actions. It's like a cosmic call for precision and efficiency in endeavors. This transit encourages you to tackle tasks with diligence and address issues with a practical mindset.

JUNE WEEK THREE

As the Moon enters Aries, your emotions take on a bold and dynamic character. It's a time of increased assertiveness and a desire to initiate new experiences. This lunar phase encourages you to embrace your individuality and pursue your passions with courage.

Jupiter square Neptune can create a sense of confusion and uncertainty. It's like a cosmic puzzle that challenges your beliefs and ideals. This aspect encourages you to critically assess your dreams and aspirations, making sure they are grounded in reality.

The Moon's ingress into Taurus brings a touch of stability and sensuality to your emotions. It's like a cosmic invitation to savor life's pleasures and find comfort in the material world. This lunar phase encourages you to nurture yourself and your loved ones.

The Sun's ingress into Cancer marks the June Solstice, a pivotal point in the year. It's a time to celebrate the arrival of summer in the Northern Hemisphere and the start of winter in the Southern Hemisphere. Cancer's energy emphasizes home, family, and emotional connections.

JUNE WEEK FOUR

⚡ Mars sextile Jupiter infuses your actions with a burst of energy and enthusiasm. It's like a cosmic call to pursue your goals with confidence and optimism. This aspect encourages you to take bold steps toward your ambitions and explore new horizons with enthusiasm.

🌑 Sun square Neptune stirs the waters of your emotions, creating a sense of confusion and uncertainty. It's like a cosmic fog that obscures your clarity. This aspect encourages you to be cautious in your decisions and seek the truth behind any illusions.

☀ Sun conjunct Jupiter is a harmonious alignment that brings a sense of expansion and good fortune. It's like a cosmic blessing, encouraging you to embrace opportunities and have faith in your abilities. This aspect fosters a positive outlook and the potential for growth and abundance.

🌙 The New Moon marks the beginning of a fresh lunar cycle, symbolizing new beginnings and a blank canvas for your intentions. It's like a cosmic reset button, allowing you to set your goals and aspirations for the coming weeks.

JUNE WEEK FOUR

🚀 Sun sextile Mars energizes your actions and drive. It's like a cosmic boost of motivation and courage. This aspect encourages you to pursue your goals with determination and assertiveness, making it an excellent time for physical activity and bold initiatives.

🦁 Mercury's ingress into Leo brings a more expressive and dramatic quality to your communication style. It's like a cosmic invitation to shine in the spotlight and share your thoughts with flair and charisma. This transit encourages creative self-expression and confident conversations.

⏱ Mercury trine Saturn promotes structured and disciplined thinking. It's like a cosmic mentor guiding your mental processes with wisdom and pragmatism. This aspect encourages you to make well-thought-out plans and approach tasks with focus and determination.

☁ Mercury trine Neptune enhances your intuition and sensitivity. It's like a cosmic bridge between the rational and the mystical. This aspect encourages artistic and spiritual pursuits and fosters empathetic and compassionate communication.

JULY WEEK ONE

☾ As the Moon moves into Scorpio, your emotions take on an intense quality. It's like a cosmic dive into the depths of your feelings and subconscious. This lunar phase encourages introspection, transformation, and a desire for authenticity in your interactions.

⚡ Venus conjunct Uranus is an electrifying cosmic connection between love and spontaneity. It's like a sudden spark in your relationships and desires. This aspect encourages you to embrace the unexpected and be open to unconventional forms of love and pleasure.

♊ Venus's move into Gemini signifies a more curious and adaptable approach to matters of the heart and aesthetics. It's like a cosmic shift in your love life, emphasizing variety and intellectual connections. This transit encourages socializing, flirting, and exploring diverse interests.

🌀 Neptune turning retrograde marks a period of introspection and inner exploration. It's like a cosmic call to review your dreams, fantasies, and spiritual connections. This aspect encourages you to look within for inspiration and to clarify your visions.

JULY WEEK ONE

♎ Venus sextile Saturn creates a harmonious balance between love and responsibility. It's like a cosmic alignment of your desires with your long-term goals. This aspect encourages stable and mature relationships and a practical approach to matters of the heart.

♐ The Moon's ingress into Sagittarius brings an adventurous and optimistic tone to your emotions. It's like a cosmic call to explore, learn, and seek higher truths. This lunar phase encourages you to embrace spontaneity and expand your horizons.

♊ Uranus's ingress into Gemini is a significant cosmic shift, bringing innovative and curious energies to your thought processes. It's like a cosmic awakening to new ideas and intellectual pursuits. This transit encourages a fresh perspective, adaptability, and open-mindedness.

♀ Venus trine Pluto is a transformative and intense connection in the realm of love and desire. It's like a cosmic alchemical process that deepens your connections and passions. This aspect encourages profound emotional experiences and a sense of empowerment in your relationships.

JULY WEEK TWO

🌙 As the Moon gracefully moves into Capricorn, the energy shifts towards a more pragmatic and disciplined emotional state. This lunar placement encourages you to take a structured approach to your feelings and responsibilities. During this phase, you may find yourself drawn to setting and achieving long-term goals, all while taking a mature and systematic approach.

🌕 The Full Moon, a celestial spectacle, marks a significant turning point in the lunar cycle. It's a powerful culmination of energy, illuminating the achievements and emotions of the preceding weeks. This phase is akin to a cosmic spotlight, casting a glow on both your successes and the areas where you need to let go. It's a moment of reflection, closure, and an opportunity to release any emotional baggage, making space for fresh intentions and new beginnings.

🌙 As the Moon dances into Aquarius, your emotions take on a more independent and innovative hue. It's as if a cosmic rebel has stirred within you, encouraging you to embrace uniqueness and unconventional experiences. During this phase, you may feel drawn to social causes, group activities, or exploring your individuality.

JULY WEEK TWO

⌛ Saturn's retrograde motion initiates a period of introspection and review of your responsibilities and long-term goals. It's like a cosmic teacher guiding you to revisit your life's structure and ensure it aligns with your authentic desires and ambitions. This phase invites you to take a step back and assess your commitments, obligations, and the path you're walking. It's a time to make adjustments and fine-tune your life plan to serve your inner aspirations better.

☾ The Moon's journey into Pisces carries you into the depths of sensitivity and empathy. It's as if a cosmic artist has painted your emotional landscape with vivid and dreamy hues. During this phase, you may find yourself more connected to the subtle undercurrents of your feelings and those of the world around you. It's a time for introspection, compassion, and a deep connection to your inner world. You may feel inspired to explore your creative side and engage with artistic or spiritual pursuits. It creates a beautifully nuanced tapestry of experiences, guiding you on your growth journey and offering insights into the ever-evolving nature of your emotions.

JULY WEEK THREE

🌙 When the Moon enters Aries, your emotional landscape experiences a dynamic awakening. Aries, a sign known for its fiery and assertive nature, infuses you with a burst of energy and initiative. It's as if a cosmic call to action stirs within your heart, urging you to embrace your adventurous side and take charge of your emotions. During this lunar phase, your passions burn brighter, and you'll find yourself drawn to challenges and new experiences. It's an ideal time to channel your enthusiasm into personal projects and pursuits.

☿ Mercury turning retrograde initiates a period of cosmic reflection and recalibration. This celestial event invites you to dive into the depths of your thoughts and communication. Mercury, the planet of communication, asks you to slow down and reconsider how you express yourself and interact with others. It's akin to a cosmic messenger urging you to revisit past conversations, clear up misunderstandings, and fine-tune your thinking. While Mercury retrograde often comes with its share of challenges, it's a valuable time for personal growth and honing your communication skills.

JULY WEEK THREE

🌙 As the Moon transitions into Taurus, your emotional realm takes on a grounded and stabilizing quality. Taurus is an earth sign associated with comfort and security. This lunar placement acts as a cosmic anchor, helping you find solace in the material world. During this phase, you may discover a deep appreciation for life's pleasures, whether that's enjoying a delicious meal, surrounding yourself with the beauty of nature, or indulging in sensory experiences that soothe your soul. The Moon in Taurus encourages you to slow down, relax, and relish the simple yet profound pleasures of life.

💕 Mercury sextile Venus creates a harmonious connection between your thoughts and emotions. It's as if your mental and emotional realms engage in a delightful dance of understanding and resonance. This aspect encourages sweet and meaningful communication, making it an ideal time for heartfelt conversations and expressions of love. Whether you're sharing your feelings with a loved one, appreciating the arts, or finding joy in creative expression, this cosmic alignment fosters harmony in your interactions and relationships.

JULY WEEK FOUR

☉ As the radiant Sun enters Leo, it's akin to a cosmic spotlight illuminating your inner performer. With Leo's proud and theatrical influence, you're encouraged to embrace your creativity, confidence, and charisma. This solar shift fuels your desire to express yourself authentically and revel in the limelight. It's your moment to showcase your unique qualities.

⚡ When the Sun forms a harmonious sextile with Uranus, prepare for a dynamic cosmic surge. This planetary alignment injects your life with excitement and innovation, akin to a sudden bolt of lightning in the night sky. It inspires you to embrace change and explore uncharted territories. Your creative thinking and adventurous spirit are sparked, making it an ideal time to venture beyond your comfort zone.

💔 Venus square Mars introduces a celestial tension between love and desire, akin to a cosmic tango where attraction and passion collide. This aspect may usher in moments of romantic friction as your desires and affections may not always align. Utilize this time to delve into the intricacies of your relationships and navigate.

JULY WEEK FOUR

🌑 The arrival of the New Moon signals a fresh cosmic beginning, akin to a blank canvas awaiting your dreams. This lunar phase prompts you to set new goals, initiate projects, and sow the seeds of your aspirations.

☉ Sun opposed Pluto heralds a period of profound transformation, resembling a cosmic confrontation between your ego and the depths of your psyche. This aspect prompts you to confront power struggles and issues of control, both within yourself and in your relationships. Though challenging, it presents an opportunity for significant personal growth and renewal.

♋ With Venus entering Cancer, your emotions and relationships step into the spotlight, enveloping you in a warm and nurturing embrace. This celestial shift encourages deeper emotional connections and intimacy.

🤝 When the Sun aligns with Mercury in conjunction, it fosters a cosmic dialogue between your inner self and your intellect. This aspect enhances your communication abilities and mental clarity.

AUGUST WEEK ONE

💔 When Venus squares Saturn, you're in for a cosmic tango between love and responsibility. It's akin to a romantic test of endurance, where the desire for affection clashes with the need for structure. This aspect can evoke feelings of restraint and limitations in your relationships. You might find yourself questioning commitments and grappling with emotional burdens. However, in navigating these challenges, you have the potential to fortify your connections. By striking a balance between the longing for love and the realities of life, you can foster enduring and meaningful partnerships.

🌙 Venus square Neptune introduces an element of dreamy ambiguity to your romantic endeavors. It's as if you're navigating through a hazy dreamscape where the boundaries between reality and illusion blur. This aspect can lead to romantic misunderstandings or idealizing someone beyond what is feasible. It's crucial to trust your intuition during this period and maintain a pragmatic perspective on love. Ensure that your emotions are anchored in truth rather than the mirages of fantasy.

AUGUST WEEK ONE

♐ With the Moon's ingress into Sagittarius, your emotions are infused with a sense of adventure and a longing for exploration. It's as though your heart seeks new experiences and craves the thrill of the unknown. This lunar placement encourages you to adopt a broader perspective and actively pursue opportunities for personal growth and learning.

♑ As the Moon moves into Capricorn, a more grounded and pragmatic emotional state prevails. It's as if a cosmic call to duty prompts you to focus on your responsibilities and long-term objectives. During this lunar phase, you may discover gratification in accomplishing tasks and making strides in your professional life. You're inclined to embrace discipline and determination to attain your goals.

♎ Mars's ingress into Libra imparts a sense of equilibrium and diplomacy to your actions. It's like an internal compass guiding you toward harmony and fairness. This cosmic transition encourages you to confront conflicts with grace and a spirit of cooperation. Your efforts to cultivate peace and sustain balance in relationships and interactions receive celestial support.

AUGUST WEEK TWO

🚀 When Mars forms a trine with Uranus, it's like igniting the engines of change and innovation in your life. This harmonious aspect aligns the fiery, assertive nature of Mars with the electrifying, unpredictable energy of Uranus. It's an excellent time for taking risks, pursuing your passions, and implementing new, bold ideas. This aspect fuels independence and strengthens your ability to initiate positive transformations.

⛔ Mars's opposition to Saturn introduces a cosmic showdown between these two powerful planets. It's as if the gas pedal and the brake pedal are pushed simultaneously. Saturn, the taskmaster of the zodiac, may create roadblocks or obstacles in your path, leading to frustration or delays. This aspect challenges you to be focused and persistent in achieving your goals.

🌝 A Full Moon is a celestial event that brings heightened emotions and culminations. It's a time when the Sun and Moon stand across from each other in the sky, highlighting the polarities in your life. Emotions are in the spotlight, and you may become aware of what needs to be released or acknowledged. Full Moons are powerful for closure and completion.

AUGUST WEEK TWO

As Mercury turns direct, it's like the gears of communication and information begin to move forward once more. The challenges and miscommunications associated with Mercury retrograde start to dissipate. This shift allows you to make more informed decisions, move forward with stalled projects, and clarify any misunderstandings. Mercury Direct offers a green light for progress and greater clarity in your daily affairs.

When Saturn forms a sextile with Uranus, it's like the cosmic forces of tradition and innovation find common ground. Saturn represents stability and structure, while Uranus symbolizes change and innovation. This harmonious aspect encourages you to blend the best of both worlds, embracing new, progressive ideas while respecting established systems. It's an excellent time for implementing positive changes in a balanced and strategic manner, leading to long-term benefits.

Venus's conjunction with Jupiter brings a touch of magic and abundance to your relationships and pleasures. It's like a cosmic blessing for matters of the heart and enjoyment. Under this influence, your capacity to attract love and beauty is magnified.

AUGUST WEEK THREE

⚡ When Mercury and Mars harmoniously sextile, it's like an intellectual adrenaline rush. Your mind becomes a finely tuned instrument of precision and clarity while your words carry a particular potency. This alignment ignites your mental engines, allowing you to tackle tasks that demand both sharp thinking and assertive action. Whether you're planning, negotiating, or engaging in conversations, you'll find that your communication has an extra punch, and your ideas hit the mark with ease.

🌙 As the Moon gracefully glides through inquisitive Gemini, it's as if the universe opens the floodgates to curiosity. Your thirst for knowledge is insatiable, and you welcome new information and ideas with open arms. This lunar influence is akin to a mental playground, perfect for diving into stimulating discussions, exploring books or courses, and relishing the richness of diverse perspectives.

✨ The encore of Mercury's sextile to Mars intensifies your mental agility and assertiveness. Your words cut through ambiguity like a laser, and your ideas are delivered with unwavering confidence.

AUGUST WEEK THREE

When the Moon shifts into Cancer, the emotional tides rise. This cosmic placement turns your focus to matters of the heart and the warmth of home. It's an ideal time to nurture your closest relationships and seek comfort in the familiar embrace of family and loved ones. It's a time when you may feel more attuned to your feelings and those of others, fostering empathy and a desire to create a warm, loving atmosphere.

The Moon's journey through vibrant Leo is like an invitation to a creative gala. Your inner artist takes the stage, beckoning you to express yourself with flair and enthusiasm. You'll find joy in showcasing your unique talents and embracing a more dramatic approach to life. It's a time to infuse every endeavor with a sense of playfulness and shine. During this time, you're drawn to self-expression, creativity, and perhaps even a touch of theatricality. The cosmic stage is set for you to share your unique talents and infuse joy into your everyday activities. It's a reminder to let your inner child play and to celebrate your individuality with exuberance.

AUGUST WEEK FOUR

☀ As the Sun enters meticulous Virgo, you're infused with a strong sense of practicality and a desire to attend to the details of life. This solar transition encourages you to focus on efficiency, health, and self-improvement. It's an excellent time for organizing, setting goals, and paying attention to the finer points in both your personal and professional life.

🌑 The arrival of the New Moon heralds a fresh start and the opportunity for new beginnings. It's like a cosmic reset button, offering a blank canvas for your intentions and goals. Take this time to set your choices for the upcoming lunar cycle, as the energy of the New Moon supports planting the seeds of your desires.

⚡ When the Sun forms a challenging square with Uranus, it's as if a bolt of cosmic electricity shakes up your routine. This aspect encourages innovation and independence but can also bring unexpected disruptions. Embrace change and be open to new ideas during this time.

💜 Venus' move into the charismatic sign of Leo brings a touch of flair to your love life and personal style.

AUGUST WEEK FOUR

Venus' harmonious trine with Saturn encourages stability and commitment in your relationships. It's an excellent period for making long-term plans and strengthening bonds.

Venus' sweet sextile to Uranus adds a dash of excitement and spontaneity to your love life. Embrace new experiences and be open to unconventional connections.

Venus' trine to Neptune creates an aura of romance and imagination. This aspect can enhance your creative and spiritual connections, bringing a dreamy quality to your relationships.

Venus' opposition to Pluto can stir up intense emotions and power struggles in your relationships. Be prepared for deep transformations in matters of the heart.

The sextile between Uranus and Neptune combines their transformative energies, opening doors to spiritual insights and creative breakthroughs. This aspect invites you to explore new dimensions of your consciousness.

SEPTEMBER WEEK ONE

Saturn's ingress into Pisces is a cosmic shift that ushers in a period of introspection and emotional exploration. During this transit, you'll find yourself delving deeper into the waters of your psyche, seeking to understand the profound undercurrents of your emotions. It's a time to embrace empathy, compassion, and a more intuitive connection with your inner self. This journey may lead to a greater understanding of your dreams and aspirations, aligning your life more closely with your spiritual path.

As Mercury makes its way into Virgo, your mental landscape becomes highly organized and detail-oriented. This alignment enhances your analytical abilities, making you a master of precision and practicality. Your keen attention to detail will serve you well in any task.

When Mercury forms a square with Uranus, your mental faculties receive an electrifying jolt of innovative thinking. Expect flashes of insight as your mind may crave change and unconventional ideas, pushing you to break free from routine thinking. This aspect encourages adaptability and openness to novel perspectives.

SEPTEMBER WEEK ONE

The Mars Jupiter square brings a surge of enthusiasm and a thirst for adventure. Your energy levels are high, and you're ready to tackle ambitious goals. However, be cautious not to overextend yourself. This aspect can lead to overzealousness, so balance your drive with practicality. When harnessed effectively, this energy can propel you toward significant achievements.

With Uranus turning retrograde, it's time to journey within. This phase invites you to revisit the changes and innovations you've experienced recently. Take a moment to integrate these insights and find deeper meaning in your life. Self-discovery and personal liberation are at the forefront during this introspective period.

The Full Moon is a powerful culmination of energy, offering an opportunity for reflection and reaping the rewards of your recent efforts. This phase calls for self-awareness and introspection, making it an excellent time to review the goals and intentions you set during the previous New Moon. Emotions may run high, so remember to channel them positively. Embrace this celestial opportunity for personal growth and self-discovery.

SEPTEMBER WEEK TWO

☾ When the Moon shifts into Aries, you'll find your emotions ignited with fiery passion and spontaneity. This cosmic ingress is a time for taking the lead and embarking on new adventures. You may feel a surge of energy and a desire to assert your individuality. It's the perfect time to start fresh, whether that means pursuing personal goals or diving into exciting initiatives.

☾ As the Moon enters Taurus, a sense of stability and practicality settles in. Your emotions gravitate towards comfort and security, making it an ideal period for indulging in life's sensual pleasures. You might find solace in the beauty of the material world and seek to enhance your financial security during this phase.

☉ The harmonious sextile between the Sun and Jupiter brings an influx of optimism and opportunity. Your confidence soars, and the world seems full of possibilities. It's a time to set your sights on ambitious goals and seize the chances for growth. This alignment encourages both personal and intellectual expansion, prompting you to explore uncharted territory with a positive mindset.

SEPTEMBER WEEK TWO

When the Moon transitions into Gemini, your curiosity is piqued, and your friendly side comes to the forefront. This period encourages you to engage in lively conversations, connect with a diverse range of people, and expand your knowledge. It's an excellent time for networking and learning, as your mind is agile and eager for new information.

Mercury's sextile with Jupiter enhances your communication and mental faculties. Your thoughts flow with ease, and you have a keen ability to convey your ideas persuasively. It's a period conducive to making big plans, whether they pertain to your personal or professional life. Learning and teaching also benefit from this aspect, so don't hesitate to share your knowledge with others.

The Sun's conjunction with Mercury aligns your thoughts and self-expression, creating a solid connection between your intellect and communication skills. Clarity and precision mark your interactions, making this an excellent time for meaningful conversations, negotiations, or any activity that requires articulate expression. Your mental acumen shines.

SEPTEMBER WEEK THREE

✹ Venus and Mars create a celestial harmony through their gentle sextile, weaving love and desire into a delightful dance. This aspect encourages a balance between passion and affection, bringing greater unity and cooperation to your relationships.

◌ Mercury's opposition with stern Saturn may pose communication challenges. This aspect can lead to misunderstandings and make it difficult to express your thoughts clearly. Patience and precision in conversations are crucial to overcome this cosmic hurdle.

✹ As Mercury moves into diplomatic Libra, your communication takes on a more balanced and cooperative tone. During this phase, you'll seek harmony in your interactions, making it an ideal time for resolving conflicts and fostering understanding.

☾ However, Mercury's opposition with Neptune can cast a dreamy and somewhat confusing veil over your thoughts. It's essential to exercise caution in your communications and pay close attention to details, as misunderstandings may arise.

SEPTEMBER WEEK THREE

🚀 Mercury's trines with Uranus and Pluto bring a surge of intellectual brilliance and transformative insights. This cosmic alignment fuels your mental agility and adaptability, freeing you from conventional thinking and allowing innovative ideas to flow.

❀ Venus enters practical Virgo, encouraging an analytical and systematic approach to matters of the heart. You'll find joy in attending to the finer details of your relationships, seeking both pleasure and perfection.

⚡ But the square between Venus and Uranus introduces an element of unpredictability in your relationships. This aspect may ignite unexpected changes and introduce unconventional romantic interests.

☀ The Sun's opposition with responsible Saturn may present challenges related to self-expression and personal authority. These obstacles will require patience and determination to overcome.

🌑 With the arrival of the New Moon, you are granted a fresh beginning. This lunar phase is your opportunity to set intentions and embark on a path of self-discovery.

SEPTEMBER WEEK FOUR

◐ Mars' entrance into Scorpio electrifies your life with a surge of intense, transformative energy. It's as if you've been handed a cosmic power tool, encouraging you to dig deep and unearth your most profound desires. This alignment sparks your determination and grit, making it a favorable time to confront challenges head-on. You'll find a wellspring of resilience and resourcefulness at your disposal.

☺ The September Equinox marks a pivotal moment in the year when day and night are in perfect equilibrium. Just as nature transitions from one season to another, this cosmic event encourages you to balance various aspects of your life. It's a reminder to adapt to life's ever-evolving circumstances and to seek equilibrium in your endeavors. This moment is the time to reevaluate your goals and realign with your true priorities.

♎ With the Sun's arrival in Libra, your focus naturally turns toward your relationships. You are inclined to seek harmony, fairness, and beauty in all interactions, both personal and professional. This period invites you to mend any imbalances, fostering a sense of equilibrium in your partnerships.

SEPTEMBER WEEK FOUR

⚡ The Sun's harmonious trines with Uranus and Pluto bestow a potent blend of transformation and innovation to your life. You become more open to change, adaptable, and resilient. This phase encourages personal growth, making you better equipped to handle life's challenges and adapt to new ideas and experiences.

☾ As the Moon progresses into Scorpio, your emotions take a profound turn. This cosmic transit is a time for introspection, a journey into your inner self to unravel deep-seated feelings and motivations. It's a period of self-discovery and a chance to understand the driving forces behind your actions.

🏔 The Moon's transition into Sagittarius introduces a sense of adventure and expansion into your emotional landscape. Your feelings take on a more open, exploratory quality. You'll be drawn to new horizons, both in your intellectual pursuits and your emotional experiences.

🔺 The Moon's entry into Capricorn shifts your focus to ambition and long-term goals. The celestial energies support your efforts, enabling you to achieve success.

OCTOBER WEEK ONE

🌑 A square between Mercury and Jupiter adds an exciting dynamic to the celestial tapestry. While the Moon in Aquarius brings an air of excitement and experimentation, this aspect can create a bit of tension. You may find yourself torn between the fine details and big-picture thinking. Your enthusiasm is palpable, but it's essential to ensure that your plans remain grounded in practicality. Finding a balance between your optimism and the specifics of your projects will be your cosmic challenge.

🌙 As the Moon gracefully pirouettes into Pisces, the emotional currents take on a dreamy and compassionate quality. Dive into creative or spiritual activities and explore the vast ocean of your inner world. Pisces encourages you to be gentle with yourself and others.

🚀 With the Moon's entry into Aries, you'll feel the cosmic engines rev up. Your energy surges, and you're ready for action. The Aries Moon is like a cosmic shot of adrenaline, propelling you to pursue goals and passions with unwavering determination. Your assertiveness and courage shine, and you have the cosmic wind at your back, making this an optimal period.

OCTOBER WEEK ONE

🕵 Mercury's move into Scorpio brings a shadowy depth to your thinking. During this phase, you're inclined to investigate matters with a magnifying glass. Superficiality won't cut it—Scorpio urges you to dig deeper and uncover hidden truths. You might become more interested in psychological and metaphysical subjects, prompting a period of intense introspection. It's a time when your intuition is heightened, guiding you through the labyrinth of complex issues.

🌕 The Full Moon rises in all its luminous glory, casting its radiant glow on your path. It is a time of culmination and realization. Reflect on the intentions you set during the New Moon and observe how they've developed. The Full Moon offers you a cosmic spotlight to see your progress and achievements. It's also an opportunity to release what no longer serves you, letting go of any emotional baggage that might be holding you back. It is a time to move forward with newfound clarity and purpose. The Full Moon marks a period of culmination and realization. Embrace the ebb and flow of these celestial tides, finding harmony between your intellectual and emotional worlds. 🌙 🚀 🔮 🌕 ✨

OCTOBER WEEK TWO

🌙 Nestling into Taurus, the Moon beckons you to ground yourself in the tangible pleasures of life. Surround yourself with the beauty of nature, indulge in delicious treats, and relish the soothing rhythms of the material world. Let this lunar phase be a gentle reminder to find joy in the simplicity of existence and appreciate the sensory delights that abound.

✦ Venus, the planet of love, engages in a delightful sextile with expansive Jupiter, casting a benevolent glow over your social sphere. This celestial alliance encourages you to open your heart, embrace generosity, and revel in the beauty of connection. It's a time when your relationships can flourish, and the bonds you share with others become a source of joy and abundance.

🌒 As the Moon transitions into communicative Gemini, the cosmic stage is set for lively intellectual exploration.

🌓 Venus, now gracing Libra, engages in a cosmic dance of opposition with steadfast Saturn. This celestial choreography urges you to balance desires and life's practicalities. While the beauty of Libra seeks harmony, Saturn's influence calls for a measured approach.

OCTOBER WEEK TWO

☾ Shifting into Cancer, the Moon invites you to immerse yourself in the waters of emotion and nurture your innermost feelings. Home and family take center stage during this lunar phase, offering a sanctuary of emotional support. Allow yourself to be attuned to the ebb and flow of your emotions, finding solace in the loving embrace of those close to you.

💜 Venus, now gracing Libra, engages in a cosmic conversation with dreamy Neptune. While this brings an air of enchantment to your relationships, it also introduces an element of ambiguity. It's a time to navigate the waters of love with gentle discernment and seek clarity amidst the romantic allure.

🔄 Pluto's direct motion signals a profound shift in the cosmic energies. It's as if the universe is encouraging you to release what no longer serves your highest good and embrace the transformative power within. This period holds the promise of inner growth and rebirth.

☽ Venus, in a harmonious trine with innovative Uranus, injects a dose of excitement. This celestial duo sparks the flame of spontaneity in matters of the heart.

OCTOBER WEEK THREE

☽ As the Moon gracefully glides into meticulous Virgo, a cosmic spotlight illuminates the details of your daily life. It's a reasonable time to bring a sense of order to your surroundings, focusing on practicalities and the finer points of your routine. Embrace a diligent approach, finding satisfaction in the precision and efficiency that can be woven into your tasks.

☉ The celestial stage is set for a cosmic clash as the radiant Sun squares off with expansive Jupiter. This alignment creates a dynamic interplay between your desire for personal growth and the need to navigate boundaries. Take heed not to overextend yourself; instead, find a balance that allows for expansion without losing sight of practical considerations.

☽ Shifting into Libra, the Moon invites you into the harmonious realms of balance and diplomacy. This lunar phase encourages you to seek equilibrium in your relationships and surroundings. Explore the beauty of compromise, aiming for a cooperative approach that fosters mutual understanding and connection.

OCTOBER WEEK THREE

◪ Mercury, the messenger of the cosmos, aligns with assertive Mars in a celestial conjunction. This powerful fusion of energy urges you to express your thoughts with confidence and assertiveness. It's a time to be bold in your communications but also to be mindful of potential conflicts that may arise from the intensity of your words.

● The cosmic ballet reaches a crescendo with the arrival of the New Moon. This lunar phase marks the beginning of a new cycle, symbolizing fresh starts and opportunities. Set intentions aligned with your deepest aspirations, and embrace the energy of renewal.

● The Moon gracefully transitions into transformative Scorpio, inviting you to explore the depths of your emotions. This lunar phase encourages introspection and a willingness to delve into the shadowy realms of your psyche. Embrace the potential for regeneration and growth that arises from acknowledging and transforming what lies beneath the surface. In this cosmic journey, the lunar shift into Scorpio invites profound introspection.

OCTOBER WEEK FOUR

🌙 Neptune's ethereal journey into Pisces ushers in a dreamy and reflective energy. This celestial shift encourages you to tap into your intuition, explore creative pursuits, and connect with the mystical dimensions of your consciousness.

☉ As the Sun embraces the transformative realms of Scorpio, a potent cosmic energy unfolds. The Sun's square with Pluto intensifies this period, urging you to delve into the depths of your psyche. It's a time of regeneration and rebirth, where shadows are illuminated, and you're invited to release what no longer serves your highest purpose.

☿ Mercury's harmonious trines with expansive Jupiter and structured Saturn create a cosmic harmony in the realm of communication and intellect. This alignment enhances your ability to express yourself with wisdom and practicality. Your thoughts are expansive yet grounded, facilitating effective decision-making and communication.

🚀 The dynamic trine between Mars and Jupiter amplifies your energy and drive.

OCTOBER WEEK FOUR

♐ Mercury's ingress into Sagittarius broadens your mental horizons, infusing your thoughts with a sense of adventure and optimism. It's a time to explore new philosophies, expand your knowledge, and embrace a more expansive view of the world.

♂ Mars' trine with Saturn brings a balance of passion and discipline to your endeavors. This cosmic alliance supports strategic and focused action, allowing you to make steady progress toward your goals. Harness this energy to build foundations and achieve long-term success.

⚡ Mercury's opposition to Uranus adds an element of surprise and innovation to your mental landscape. Be open to unexpected insights and breakthroughs, and embrace the potential for original thinking and unconventional solutions.

♇ Mercury's sextile with transformative Pluto empowers your communication with depth and influence. Your words carry a magnetic force, allowing you to navigate power dynamics with finesse and bring about meaningful transformations.

NOVEMBER WEEK ONE

🌙 The Moon's entrance into Aries heralds a burst of dynamic energy and initiative. You may find yourself motivated to embark on new projects or embrace a more assertive and independent approach.

💔 Venus squares Jupiter, creating a cosmic tension between the planet of love and beauty and the expansive influence of Jupiter. This aspect suggests the need for balance in relationships. Be mindful of extravagance or overindulgence, and seek harmony in your connections without overpromising.

🚀 As Mars forms a harmonious trine with Neptune, a wave of inspired action and creativity permeates your pursuits. Your energy aligns with a higher sense of purpose, allowing you to infuse your actions with imagination and spirituality. It's a favorable time for artistic expression and projects driven by passion.

🔥 Mars strides into Sagittarius, igniting a fire within your pursuits. This cosmic alignment brings enthusiasm, adventurous spirit, and a desire for exploration. Embrace the call to broaden your horizons and infuse your actions with the optimism of Sagittarian energy.

NOVEMBER WEEK ONE

⚡ Mars opposes Uranus, generating a surge of unpredictable and rebellious energy. This aspect encourages you to break free from limitations, but it's crucial to navigate change with awareness. Use this dynamic force wisely, avoiding impulsive actions that may lead to unnecessary conflicts.

○ The Full Moon illuminates the sky, casting its glow on your emotions and experiences. This moment is a potent time for self-reflection, releasing what no longer serves you, and celebrating achievements. The energy of the Full Moon encourages you to embrace emotional fulfillment and find balance in your life.

☾ Mars sextile Pluto adds depth and intensity to your actions. This cosmic alliance empowers you to pursue your goals with determination and resilience. It's a transformative period where you can harness your inner strength to overcome challenges and make lasting changes.

♊ The Moon's ingress into Gemini shifts the focus to communication and intellectual pursuits. It is excellent for learning and engaging in conversations.

NOVEMBER WEEK TWO

🌀 Brace yourself for a seismic cosmic shift as the rebellious planet Uranus gracefully waltzes into Taurus, heralding a period of groundbreaking change in the realms of stability and security. This celestial phenomenon invites you to embrace a revolutionary mindset, encouraging flexibility and openness to innovative ideas that can reshape your foundations.

💔 The cosmic drama intensifies with Venus square Pluto, a celestial tango delving into the profound transformations within relationships. This powerful aspect acts as a cosmic crucible, challenging you to confront and overcome obstacles, paving the way for a profound rebirth in matters of the heart.

☾ As the Moon gracefully glides into the nurturing waters of Cancer, emotions take center stage. This gentle energy encourages a focus on self-care, urging you to connect with your intuitive, feeling side. It's a cosmic invitation to seek solace in the comforts of home and find emotional refuge in the embrace of loved ones. This nurturing energy invites you to prioritize self-care, nurturing your intuitive and feeling side.

NOVEMBER WEEK TWO

🔄 Mercury takes center stage in its retrograde journey, prompting a cosmic intermission for introspection and review. It's time to revisit old projects, relationships, and unresolved issues. Exercise caution in communication, expect delays and use this period for a thoughtful reevaluation of the past.

🦁 The lunar spotlight shifts to Leo, infusing the cosmic scene with creative flair and self-expression. This phase encourages you to tap into your inner performer, engage in activities that bring joy, and radiate your authentic light, adding a touch of celestial glamour to your endeavors.

🔍 Jupiter, the cosmic magnifier, takes a reflective pause as it turns retrograde. This cosmic realignment invites you to reassess personal beliefs, philosophies, and growth goals. Use this celestial respite for inner exploration, refining your path with newfound wisdom.

🤝 The cosmic conversation amps up as Mercury forms a dynamic conjunction with Mars. This alignment infuses communication with assertive energy and mental agility.

NOVEMBER WEEK THREE

As Mercury forms a sextile with Pluto, the cosmic energies stimulate profound insights and transformative conversations. Your mental faculties are sharp, making it an ideal time for research, investigation, and delving into the depths of your thoughts.

Mercury's ingress into Scorpio intensifies your communication style. Your words carry emotional depth and intensity, and you're drawn to explore profound subjects. This transit encourages authenticity and a willingness to engage in meaningful dialogue.

Mercury trine Neptune adds a touch of intuition and creative inspiration to your mental landscape. Your imagination is vivid, and you may find expressing yourself through artistic or spiritual channels particularly fulfilling.

With the arrival of the New Moon, a cosmic reset occurs. It's a potent time for setting intentions, initiating new projects, and aligning your energy with fresh beginnings. Reflect on your desires and plant the seeds for future growth.

NOVEMBER WEEK THREE

☉ Sun conjunct Mercury in Scorpio intensifies your communication style. Your words carry weight and emotional depth, making it a favorable time for expressing profound thoughts and engaging in meaningful discussions.

♐ Mercury's ingress into Sagittarius brings a shift in mental focus. Your thoughts expand, and you may find yourself drawn to broader perspectives, higher learning, and philosophical discussions.

🔄 The harmonious dance of Uranus sextile Neptune introduces an innovative and visionary energy. This cosmic alignment encourages you to blend intuition with intellect, fostering creative and groundbreaking ideas.

⚡ As the Sun opposes Uranus, expect a surge of unpredictable energy. This aspect challenges the status quo, urging you to embrace change and innovation. Be open to possibilities and unconventional approaches.

🌊 The Sun trine Neptune brings a sense of inspiration and spiritual insight. Your intuition is heightened, and you may find beauty in connecting with your dreams and inner visions.

NOVEMBER WEEK FOUR

 The cosmic journey begins as the Sun steps into Sagittarius, bringing a burst of adventurous energy. Under Sagittarius' influence, curiosity reigns, and the quest for knowledge takes center stage. Your focus shifts to explore new horizons, seek novel experiences, and revel in the joy of discovery. Embrace the fiery passion within, letting the cosmic archer guide you toward uncharted possibilities.

 Experience an intellectual expansion as Mercury trines Jupiter, opening your mind to grand ideas. This celestial conversation encourages learning and teaching on a broader scale. Positive thinking prevails, and you're better equipped to see the bigger picture. Seize this cosmic synergy to explore new concepts, communicate with optimism, and embrace enthusiasm for intellectual pursuits.

 Transformative energies abound as the Sun sextiles Pluto, empowering your journey. This celestial aspect taps into your inner strength, allowing you to make positive life changes. Overcome challenges with resilience and influence your circumstances positively.

NOVEMBER WEEK FOUR

🌈 Bask in the abundance of joy with the harmonious trine between Venus and Jupiter. This celestial dance invites you to indulge in life's finer things, expanding your capacity for love and enjoyment.

♎ Find stability and commitment in your relationships as Venus trines Saturn. This cosmic harmony emphasizes building lasting foundations in matters of the heart and artistic pursuits. Your connections deepen, and creative projects gain structure and longevity under this celestial influence. Cultivate enduring bonds during this cosmic embrace.

🔄 Saturn turns direct, signaling a shift in cosmic energies. Progress is palpable in areas where you've diligently worked towards your goals. With Saturn's forward motion, adopt a disciplined and steady approach to your ambitions, moving forward with newfound clarity and purpose.

✦ Communication flows as Mercury turns direct, lifting the fog of retrograde energies. Delays and misunderstandings begin to resolve.

DECEMBER WEEK ONE

☾ A shift in the cosmic dance occurs as the Moon gracefully enters Taurus, casting a tranquil and stabilizing energy over your emotional landscape. Like a serene melody, Taurus encourages you to indulge in sensory pleasures, grounding yourself in comfort and savoring the beauty that surrounds you. Take this time to nurture your senses and find solace in simple joys.

♥ Venus extends a celestial invitation as it forms a harmonious sextile with Pluto. This cosmic alignment sparks magnetic energy in matters of love, infusing your relationships with intensity and depth. Allow yourself to explore the transformative power of connection, delving into the emotional richness that Venus and Pluto together bestow upon your romantic endeavors.

☾ The Moon gracefully glides into Gemini, ushering in a dynamic and communicative energy. The cosmic twins inspire curiosity and versatility, encouraging you to embrace diverse perspectives and engage in lively conversations. It's a time to express your thoughts with the agility that Gemini brings to your emotional world.

DECEMBER WEEK ONE

🌕 The Full Moon graces the celestial stage, casting its luminous glow and illuminating the skies. This decisive lunar phase brings culmination and fulfillment to projects or intentions set during the New Moon. Emotions run high, and you may find clarity in the moonlight, guiding you to release what no longer serves you and celebrate the achievements of your lunar journey.

🌙 Nestle into the nurturing embrace of Cancer as the Moon finds its way into this tender zodiac sign. Cancer's energy encourages you to prioritize emotional well-being, seeking comfort in the safety of home and the warmth of close connections. Allow your feelings to flow like the gentle tide, creating a soothing rhythm that restores your emotional equilibrium.

☾ Mercury forms a harmonious trine with Neptune, creating a dreamy and imaginative atmosphere. Your thoughts become infused with poetic inspiration, and communication takes on a more intuitive and compassionate tone. Dive into the depths of your creative pursuits, letting the cosmic currents of Mercury and Neptune guide your expressions.

DECEMBER WEEK TWO

♂ As the celestial battlefield unfolds, Mars squares off against Saturn, casting a cosmic struggle between the fiery desire for action and the stern discipline of limitations. This cosmic clash encourages you to navigate challenges with a blend of assertiveness and patience, fostering resilience in the face of obstacles.

☽ The Moon gracefully pirouettes into analytical Virgo, casting a spotlight on precision and practicality in your emotional realm. It's an ideal time to scrutinize your feelings, organize your thoughts, and approach tasks with a meticulous touch.

☉ Neptune, the Dreamweaver, resumes its direct journey, lifting the mist from your aspirations. Your dreams gain clarity, and the ethereal realms beckon, inspiring a deeper connection to your spiritual compass.

⚡ Mercury, the cosmic messenger, engages in a dynamic tango of opposition with rebellious Uranus. This celestial conversation electrifies your thoughts, introducing unexpected twists and turns. Embrace the mental excitement and dare to think outside the conventional box.

DECEMBER WEEK TWO

◪ Mercury's harmonious trine with Neptune bestows a touch of enchantment upon your communication style. Your words become a conduit for empathy and creativity, fostering a profound connection with those around you.

♐ Expanding the horizons of thought, Mercury gallops into adventurous Sagittarius, encouraging a broader perspective and a thirst for knowledge. Your mind becomes a wanderer, exploring the vast landscapes of philosophy and wisdom.

♎ The Moon pirouettes into Libra, donning the robes of harmony. Relationships take center stage, and the cosmic energies favor diplomacy and fairness. Seek equilibrium in your emotional interactions and appreciate the beauty of balanced connections.

◪ Mercury's harmonious sextile with Pluto empowers your words with depth and intensity. Engage in transformative conversations, delving into the profound and revealing aspects of your psyche.

DECEMBER WEEK THREE

🌑 The enigmatic Moon slips into the intense waters of Scorpio, beckoning you to explore the depths of your emotions. It's a time for introspection, where hidden feelings may surface, guiding you on a journey of self-discovery.

☉ The Sun squares off against Saturn, a cosmic challenge that tests your resilience and commitment. This celestial configuration prompts a review of your goals and structures. Patience and perseverance become your guiding lights as you navigate obstacles with wisdom and fortitude.

♐ The Moon ventures into adventurous Sagittarius, ushering in a sense of optimism and exploration. Embrace a spirit of curiosity, allowing your emotions to soar into uncharted territories. Seek out new experiences that broaden your horizons.

🌑 A New Moon graces the cosmic stage, offering a blank canvas for new beginnings. Set your intentions for the upcoming lunar cycle, envisioning the path you wish to tread. It is a potent time for planting the seeds of your aspirations.

DECEMBER WEEK THREE

● The elusive Black Moon tiptoes into Sagittarius, bringing an air of mystery to your quest for truth. Delve into the realms of knowledge and spirituality, uncovering hidden insights that guide you on your journey.

◫ The December Solstice heralds a shift in cosmic energies as the Sun enters Capricorn. It marks a turning point, inviting you to reflect on the past year and set intentions for the months ahead. Embrace the rebirth of light and the promise of new beginnings.

♑ With the Sun now in Capricorn, the cosmic spotlight illuminates your ambitions and responsibilities. Take stock of your achievements and lay the groundwork for future success. Your determination and hard work become potent allies.

◾ Sun squares Neptune, casting a dreamy aura over your reality. While creativity and intuition are heightened, tread carefully in practical matters. Ensure your dreams are anchored in truth, avoiding illusions that may lead you astray.

DECEMBER WEEK FOUR

💜 As Venus engages in a cosmic dance with Neptune, beautifully intricate yet potentially intricate energy surrounds matters of the heart. The lines between reality and illusion might blur, emphasizing the importance of careful discernment in navigating relationships. Be cautious about idealizing situations or individuals excessively, and strive for clarity in your emotional connections.

✦ Venus gracefully transitions into the organized realm of Capricorn, bringing a sense of structure and responsibility to your expressions of love and appreciation for beauty. During this phase, practical considerations may play a significant role in your romantic pursuits, encouraging you to establish strong foundations. Considerate gestures of love can be particularly impactful during this period.

☾ The Moon glides into the dreamy waters of Pisces, inviting you to explore the poetic landscapes of emotion and intuition. This celestial alignment heightens your sensitivity and compassion, creating an ideal moment for artistic endeavors, meditation, or introspective journeys to connect with your inner self.

DECEMBER WEEK FOUR

♣ Traverse the celestial realms as the Moon gracefully moves into the earthy embrace of Taurus. Immerse yourself in the decadent pleasures of the material world, finding tranquility and stability in the comforting embrace of your surroundings. Revel in the sensory delights that bring a sense of grounding and peace.

☐ Engage in a celestial dance as Mercury engages in a nuanced tussle with Saturn, creating an intricate interplay between communication and structure. Navigate this cosmic tension with thoughtful and deliberate expression, being attuned to potential challenges in conveying your ideas. Embrace patience and diligence in your communication, using this time as an opportunity to refine your thoughts and concepts.

◪ Witness the Moon's elegant pirouette into the inquisitive realms of Gemini, igniting intellectual curiosity and elevating your communication skills. Explore the boundless landscape of ideas and relish the adaptability that this lunar phase bestows upon your mental pursuits. Embrace the art of intellectual exploration with open-mindedness and enthusiasm.

NOTES

NOTES

NOTES

Astrology, Tarot & Horoscope Books.

Mystic Cat

www.ingramcontent.com/pod-product-compliance
Lightning Source LLC
LaVergne TN
LVHW051844080426
835512LV00018B/3057